DONNIE WAHLBERG

and

DANNY WOOD

of the

NEW KIDS ON THE BLOCK

By Eartha Glass

Modern Publishing
A Division of Unisystems, Inc.
New York, New York 10022

Book Design by Bob Feldgus

CONTENTS

PART 1
DONALD E. WAHLBERG

Growing Up in Dorchester 5
Being Discovered 10
A Band Is Born 14
The Bumpy Road to Success 17
Donnie Data 21

PART 2
DANIEL W. WOOD

Family and School Life 24
Danny's Choice. 29
Getting It Together 32
The Right Stuff 35
Danny Data. 38

PART 3
NEW KIDS RULE

Onstage 43
Lovin' NKOTB Forever 46
Around the World. 49
Taking It Step by Step 52
On the Horizon and Into the '90s 54
Music and Videos 58
Awards and Honors. 59
On Tour 60

Donnie has always loved attention—whether from his family, friends or fans! Janet Macoska

PART 1

DONALD E. WAHLBERG

GROWING UP IN DORCHESTER

Donald Wahlberg describes himself as a very serious person. "I've been described as an intellectual, but I've also been described as a basket case," says the twenty-one-year-old. "I fall right in the middle of—somewhere between an intellectual and a schizo."

Donnie is a real intriguing guy. He is complex and simple at the same time. Guess that's why so many gals are head over heels in love with this New Kid On The Block!

When Donald Wahlberg was born on August 17, 1969, in Boston, Massachusetts to proud parents, Alma and Donald, Sr., no one in the Wahlberg family had any idea that by the age of fourteen, this bundle of joy would be on his way to international fame.

If there's one thing that little Donnie never lacked, it was company. He got plenty of it from his three sisters —Debbie, Michelle, Tracy—and big brothers Arthur,

The name, New Kids On The Block, came from a song that Donnie helped to write for their very first album. Eddie Malluk/Retna

Paul, James, and Robert. Soon, Donnie had another playmate to frolic with when the youngest Wahlberg, Mark, was born.

It certainly wasn't easy raising nine kids, but Mr. and Mrs. Wahlberg had patience galore. "My father was a union man and my mother was a nurse," says Donnie. "My mother doesn't have to work anymore." Donald, Sr., worked hard driving a truck, while Alma worked at St. Margaret's Hospital. The Wahlbergs lived in the Dorchester section of Boston in a small modest house. Trying to make ends meet was challenging, and the Wahlbergs did go through some rough times.

Donnie's parents encouraged the children to be open-minded, self-confident, considerate of others, and to express their opinions freely. From the start, Donnie learned to be positive—a word that pops up more than once when chatting with him. "My parents inspired 'positivity' in me," says Donnie.

Growing up in such a large family helped Donnie learn how to get along with others and how to share. Donald, Sr., and Alma also were very big on togetherness. With nine kids, you wouldn't think that all of them got together regularly, but Mom Alma made sure the family always ate dinner together. In addition to going to church every Sunday, the family also played bingo together every week. The Wahlbergs were parishioners at St. Gregory's church in Boston where Donnie received his First Holy Communion at the age of seven.

When asked his feelings about being from such a big family, Donnie said, "It's the best! There's always someone to hang out with or talk to about your problems. You're never depressed." Donnie has great respect for his parents and is very thankful for all of their support.

Since expensive toys were few in the Wahlberg household, Donnie and his brothers occupied themselves with sports. They often played basketball in nearby city schoolyards. Although Donnie loves shooting some hoops—as all the New Kids do—before taking the stage to perform a show, Donnie has a special place in his heart for baseball. In fact, Donnie says his first ambition was "to be a baseball star."

Although the Wahlberg kids generally got along great, there was the occasional sibling battle. Donnie became closest to his baby brother Mark and the two stuck together even when their older brothers occasionally tried to bully them.

When arguments broke out among the Walhberg kids, it was Donnie who always tried to smooth things over. Communication is always the best solution in Donnie's book. He often played peacemaker by getting his brothers and sisters to talk their problems out. Of the five New Kids On The Block, Donnie is known as the "peace-lovin'" Kid!

This peaceful side of Donnie was nourished by his early educational years. Although the Dorchester section of Boston was home to people of many colors and nationalities, other areas of Boston were strictly white.

"We grew up when they were trying to integrate the schools with busing," recalls Donnie. "A lot of bad stuff came up—a lot of racism. But kids weren't involved with it."

At the time, Donnie was entering kindergarten. Unlike some parents, Donnie's mother felt that he would benefit from being exposed to children of other races and cultures. So, come that fall, Donnie grabbed his lunch, waved goodbye to his mother, and went off to William Monroe Trotter School, located in a tough section of Boston called Roxbury (Bobby Brown's hometown). It was more than a half hour ride each way for Donnie, but he didn't mind. This adorable little blond-haired boy was very excited about learning and making new friends.

Always fond of talking, Donnie made quite a few friends. Many of the children were black and they introduced Donnie to rap music and some intense dance moves.

Donnie spent much of his spare time hanging out on the streets with his new friends. He started to lip-sync to rap songs and repeated raps that his friends wrote. Eventually, Donnie started to write some impressive raps of his own!

One of the friends Donnie made at William Monroe Trotter was a boy named Danny Wood who also loved to rap and dance. Danny and Donnie became fast friends and used to spend many an afternoon chilling on the streets. They got into breakdancing with the rest of their pals, and they practiced their raps in the halls, on the street, on the bus, in their rooms—everywhere!

Donnie used to lip synch to rap songs before he began writing his own.
Ernie Paniccioli

Donnie's mother was always supportive of her children's endeavors. Although rap music was something new to her, she was open to it, and liked the way it stimulated Donnie's creativity. Maybe that's why Donnie has such an open mind today when it comes not only to music, but world issues such as racism.

When asked about his faults, Donnie is quick with a response. "One of my faults is I try to make everyone happy, which ends up making half the people sad because I can't make everyone happy," he explains. "And sometimes it ends up making me sad. My mother is the same way—I think that's where I got it from. Like when I go home on vacation, I try and spend time with every person I know and I always leave someone hangin'. You can only spread yourself so far. I'm not butter, but it makes me feel bad."

9

BEING
DISCOVERED

Donnie's interest in music continued to grow. Although he never was really concerned that much with singing, he was pretty disappointed when he didn't make the William Monroe Trotter School Chorus. Danny was selected and so were two kids that Donnie was starting to become friendly with—Jonathan and Jordan Knight. Donnie remembers that the Knight brothers had really excellent voices.

So, Donnie busied himself with other aspects of music—playing drums, dancing, and rapping.

While Danny and the rest of his chums were singing their "do-re-mi's," Donnie decided to have some fun of his own. At the ripe old age of ten, Donnie formed a band called Risk with some other kids. "We were really terrible," Donnie admits. However, at the time, Donnie and his bandmates thought they were the greatest group going. Risk held band practice under Donnie's porch, and Donnie rapped and banged away on his homemade drum kit like there was no tomorrow!

By the time Donnie entered Phyllis Wheatley Middle School with his pal Danny, Michael Jackson fever had begun to sweep the nation. Donnie loved Michael Jackson's music and thought he was the absolute coolest! The Moonwalk was catching on, and Donnie was taken with how neat his idol looked doing the swift moves on stage. Donnie started to practice the Moonwalk and to impersonate Michael J. in his room. He even had a Michael look-alike outfit! (F.Y.I.: Jordan Knight used to impress everyone in his elementary school by Moonwalking through the school's halls.)

Eventually, Donnie and Danny began attending

Copley Square High School where Donnie made the school's baseball team. Donnie, Danny, and some other kids they used to hang out with dubbed themselves the Kool Aid Bunch. The group was about just chilling out and doing what they liked best—rapping and dancing, and soon they started to make a name for themselves. Naturally, girls thought that Donnie, Danny, and the rest of the guys were pretty cute, and Donnie loved the attention.

The Kool Aid Bunch gave Donnie confidence. He auditioned for the school's drama club, and landed roles in several school productions and plays. He discovered that he really enjoyed entertaining people and putting on a good show.

As far as first crushes go, Donnie recalls that special experience. "I guess the first was this girl in Boston called Wanda when I was fifteen or sixteen," he begins. "Wanda Pumpernickle. It's the truth. I loved her and she left me for another man. I cried a lot, but she cries now ha, ha."

Although many people think that it was always in this New Kid's heart to be as successful as he is today in the music world, Donnie says it came as a big surprise to him. Growing up in Dorchester, Donnie had other things on his mind.

"When I was little, I wasn't thinking about being a star," reveals Donnie, frankly. "Know what I'm saying? I was thinking, 'How am I gonna get through tomorrow with fifteen cents in my pocket and dealing with the bullies down the street?' That's what I was thinking about. I wasn't starstruck and trying to be a star."

When that memorable day came in the summer of 1984, Donnie had no idea what was going to happen. He was tipped off by a friend about some auditions for a dance group being held by a man named Maurice Starr and talent manager Mary Alford. Donnie wasn't even

Because Donnie didn't believe his voice was good enough, he almost didn't even audition for the NKOTB. Ernie Paniccioli

sure if he wanted to audition for them. Thinking his voice wasn't all that good, Donnie decided not to go. Then suddenly, just like that, he changed his mind and headed over to where the auditions were being held.

Of course, Donnie was scared and nervous, but he just walked through the door and stood in front of Maurice Starr, the mastermind behind New Edition and the same genius who would soon unleash the gift within each New Kid On The Block. When asked exactly what happened at that crucial meeting—the day New Kids On The Block officially was born—Donnie fills with emotion and warmth.

"Maurice just asked me my name and how old I was," recalls Donnie, smiling sweetly. "He asked me, 'So, what do you like to do?' I said, 'I like to rap and I like to dance.' Maurice said, 'You like to rap, then get out there and rap.' I said, 'I need some music.' He said, 'All right,' and started clapping his hands. I started rapping and I went on and on and on and just kept rapping and just kept rapping.

"He told me at the time, 'You're the best rapper I've seen.' Everything I did, I just made up on the spot. I could rap on the train, rap on the trolleys, rap at school and just do it for fun. But for this guy, who had been producing groups like New Edition, to tell me, 'Hey, you're a talented kid—you're one of the best rappers that I've heard'—that, to me, meant that I'm not just a kid off the street—I'm really something."

Donnie and the rest of the New Kids consider Maurice more than just the band's writer and producer. Their feelings for Maurice run deep. Donnie stresses that he's their friend above all else. When the Kids were scouting for a record deal, they were approached by a major record company who insisted that Maurice Starr could only produce four tracks on the album.

"We said, 'NO!'" explains Donnie. "This record company was like our last hope, but we said no because we would never leave Maurice. It is a personal thing. Maurice is one of my best friends and that's what it's always going to be about."

Donnie's love for Maurice Starr is very spirited. Whenever Maurice's name comes up in conversation, Donnie can't seem to say enough about him and all that he's done for him, Danny, Jordan, Jon, and Joe McIntyre. Maurice Starr changed all of the New Kids' lives. "He's more than just a guy who created something," says Donnie. "He's a guy who brought out something inside me and all of the members of New Kids On The Block. It was in there, but we were too nervous or we just didn't take it seriously. It changed my life. I'll be grateful to him—not so much for being behind us and producing our music and trying to help make us what we are today—that's great—but for being such a kind and incredible person."

A BAND IS BORN

After Donnie's audition for Maurice, he sent a message to Jon and Jordan Knight, whose "good voices" he remembered from elementary school, and asked them to try out for the band. They auditioned and got in right away.

Then, Donnie met up with his good buddy, Danny, and told him all about Maurice's musical project. Danny, however, took a little more convincing than Jordan and Jon.

The youngest and only blue-eyed New Kid, Joe McIntyre, was not friends with any of the others. After a pal of Donnie's named Jamie Kelley left the band because his parents didn't want him exposed to show business at such a young age, Maurice went looking for a replacement. He wanted someone who was younger than the other four and he wanted a boy with a high-pitched voice. On Father's Day, 1985, a twelve-year-old Irish-American boy from Jamaica Plain named Joe McIntyre auditioned for Maurice. Joe must have sung pretty well because he was asked to join immediately! The adorable New Kids On The Block were ready for action!

Although they're extremely close now, New Kids On The Block weren't always a family. Donnie, Danny, Jon, and Jordan had known each other for years and had gotten friendly with Jamie. Although Joe had nothing to do with Jamie's decision to leave the band, the others still resented Joe for replacing their pal.

"We didn't know Joe because he was from a different neighborhood," says Donnie. "He looked kind of 'square'—but he eventually fit in well. We love him, we accept him, he's cool."

Although Joe felt funny, too, at times, he didn't let any of this faze him. He just let his sweet personality

Boston's, and almost everyone's, favorite five (left to right): Jordan Knight, Danny Wood, Joe McIntyre, Jonathan Knight, and Donnie Wahlberg. Todd Kaplan, Star File

shine through, and soon the other guys took the time to understand and accept him.

It's not known for certain if it was that particular incident with Joe that taught Donnie a lesson about judging others before getting to know them, but today, this is a situation Donnie speaks of often.

"To not have an open mind is to be ignorant and that's the biggest problem with America," explains twenty-one-year-old Donnie. "A lot of people are ignorant. I'm not using that in a derogatory way because ignorance is strictly a lack of knowledge. So, people who are ignorant should take the time to learn about things and then they will not be ignorant anymore. Don't judge people

15

of another color until you know people of another color. And don't judge me until you know about me."

Once the band was recruited, they knew that they had plenty of hard work ahead of them. They were all still in school so sticking to rehearsal schedules was no easy task. Donnie not only went to school, but had a part-time job *and* rehearsed every single day with the band. We're talking about a guy who's ambitious enough to study the Chinese language in high school!

In the beginning, nobody really knew what to expect. Maurice had a concept, but he wasn't exactly sure where it would take him. "I wanted a white New Edition," explains New Kids' creator Starr. "I wanted the Osmonds with soul. I wanted kids who had a raw look, not who looked like models. It's a more interesting look."

Maurice decided to call the group Nynuk, which he defines as "love throughout the nations." He experimented with songs, musical compositions, choreography, and even the group's wardrobe. Meanwhile, the Kids practiced until their dance steps were smooth and slick. Their "debut" in 1985 was a show at the Joseph Lee School in Dorchester, Massachusetts. Jon, Jordan, Danny, Joe and Donnie not only had to focus their attention on their fancy footwork, but had to make sure to keep up with the music because they were lip-syncing to a tape. Maurice, who knows how to play quite a few instruments, served as the New Kids' pre-recorded band.

After Donnie finished high school (with a tutor), things started coming together. They changed their name to New Kids On The Block, taking the name from the title of a song from their first album.

THE BUMPY ROAD
TO
SUCCESS

After Donnie, Danny, Jordan, Jon, and Joe spent countless hours in the recording studio working very closely with Maurice Starr, the debut album from New Kids On The Block was ready to be shipped! The year was 1986 and spring was in the air. In April, the album, *New Kids On The Block,* was available in record stores. The first single from the record was "Be My Girl." The Kids were extremely pumped up for the release and had high hopes for their debut, but the album did not receive the attention that they had hoped for. In the ocean of record releases, the New Kids' debut made but a minor splash. Other singles, "Stop It Girl," and "Didn't I (Blow Your Mind)?," followed, but all went virtually unnoticed.

Looking back, Donnie can see some problems with the album. "I mean, we had Maurice to guide us, but we really came out of nowhere...and it took us a long time to develop our talents," he explains. "I listen to some of my parts on the first album and it's like—I was terrible!"

In spite of the fact that the album did not get off the ground and climb the charts, the New Kids concentrated on performing. They wanted to let America know who and what the New Kids On The Block were about. Oldest New Kid, Jon, remembers, "We've really pushed ourselves on people—in the early days we'd do everything from playing clubs to singing at the Statue of Liberty on the Fourth of July—and it's paid off."

Sometimes, when the Kids were busy "pushing themselves on people," some people pushed back. During one of their earlier shows, when the Kids were

17

Donnie describes himself as "kind, giving, and tons of fun" as well as "very impatient." Larry Busacca/Retna Ltd.

dressed in matching bright gold and silver outfits, they were booed off the stage. That sure is hard to believe!

The Kids hoped for success, and though they had some rough times, they never let go of their dreams. Maurice, who learned as a youth that you have to hold on tight to your dreams and hopes, helped the guys stay optimistic.

As a child, Maurice Starr (his real name is Larry Johnson) wanted he and his brothers to become as famous as The Jackson Five. When the Johnson Brothers decided to call it quits, Maurice concentrated on a solo career and eventually released his debut album, *Flaming Starr,* on RCA Records. The album sank to the bottom of the charts, but Maurice refused to give up on his dream and decided to pursue his interest in producing. It's a good thing, too! If Maurice had given up his dream of a career in music, then the world would never have known such awesome acts as New Edition, Bobby Brown, New Kids On The Block, and many more to come!

Often, Maurice would sit down with the Kids and have heart-to-heart chats about their future. It was very difficult for the Kids because they were so young at the time. When things hadn't taken off immediately, naturally the thought that maybe it was all a waste of time entered their minds. In fact, Donnie's younger brother, Mark, an original New Kids recruit, dropped out after six months, supposedly because he was more interested in playing basketball than being in a band.

The Kids' parents certainly worried about the future of the band, but Maurice reassured them. Donnie's mother, Alma, remembers her first encounter with Maurice: "He dazzled me. He told me they would be the biggest thing ever—as big as the Beatles." Truth is, Maurice wasn't too far off with his forecast!

In 1988, Columbia Records released *Hangin' Tough.*

Single after single was released—without success. And then, in a stroke of luck, radio station WRBQ-FM in Tampa, Florida decided to start playing the New Kids' fourth single, "Please Don't Go Girl" on the air. Soon, other pop radio stations followed suit and added the single to their playlists. As Joe's sweet voice crooned "Please Don't Go Girl" over radios all across America, the New Kids, their families, and Maurice saw a rosy future ahead for the young band!

Maurice borrowed $12,000 from his mother to make a promotional video for the single. In a snap, "Please Don't Go Girl" shot up to the No. 10 slot on the charts. *Hangin' Tough* also launched "You Got It (The Right Stuff)," "Hangin' Tough," "I'll Be Lovin' You (Forever)," and "Cover Girl." In no time at all, *Hangin' Tough* climbed from the bottom of the charts straight to the top of the charts! The New Kids' debut album, which got zero attention back in 1986, was re-released in 1989. Teens everywhere were re-discovering the New Kids' first album. The seeds of New Kids mania had sprouted!

The biggest break that the New Kids got was probably the chance to open for Tiffany. Interrupting the pop star's lunch, the Kids marched into her dressing room and gave her a sampling of their live show. Needless to say, Tiffany was quite impressed.

"When we started our first tour with Tiffany it was like we had to prove ourselves," recalls Donnie. "It wasn't that we had to prove it to her—she was great and she was nice from day one. We had something to prove to America."

And did they ever! New Kids On The Block proved to the world they have "the right stuff!"

DONNIE DATA

When the fans scream their approval, Donnie goes crazy onstage. "Performing makes me happy, whether it's for 50,000 people—or five!" reveals Donnie. "I think I was born to be on a stage. No joke!"

Donnie is definitely a "take-charge" type of guy. He loves to be the leader. For example, if the Kids are doing a photo session and one of them is ignoring the camera, Donnie will tell them to pay attention. If there's a problem, he'll try to work it through. In fact, this concerned New Kid once said that he'd like to meet Mikhail Gorbachev (leader of the Soviet Union), so they could talk about giving peace a chance! It follows that Donnie's favorite saying is "Peace out!"

When asked about his best and worst qualities, Donnie responded: "I'm kind, giving and tons of fun!" and "I'm very impatient! I love talking and I'm always thinking. I love to be in love!" Jon says that Donnie is a real charmer who often gives gals compliments about their eyes and smiles. Joe admits that when he first met Donnie, he was a little scared of him because of his "wild" reputation. But as Joe got to know Donnie, he began to appreciate him more and more, and realized that there are many facets to Donnie's incredible personality!

When it comes to dating, down-to-earth Donnie digs a girl with a strong personality who likes to have fun and who is very independent. And this New Kid's idea for the perfect date? "A walk and dinner at a quiet restaurant, and a movie." Donnie stresses that he likes privacy and a very relaxed atmosphere. Donnie is the type of guy who likes to spend quiet evenings at home. He also has said that since he comes from such a big family, he hopes to eventually have a big family himself someday.

Some of Donnie's favorite things include: *Sesame*

No doubt they're a family—Donnie (right) with his mom and brother Mark. Ernie Paniccioli

Street, Oreo cookies, the colors black and gold, actor Al Pacino, actress Cher, the movies *Scarface* and *The Godfather,* his dad's cooking, performing on stage, baseball and basketball, the book *Old Yeller,* his family, dance music, drawing and peace! Donnie also likes the yellow part of an egg! "I order my eggs sunny side up, so I can dip my toast in the yolk," reveals Donnie. "I eat everything on my plate first, and then I take one piece of toast, scoop up the yolk and eat it. It tastes so good!"

Among Donnie's not-so-favorites: technical difficulties when the Kids are performing, fans who run up behind him and cut his hair for a souvenir, close-mindedness, prejudice, war, stereotypes and people who judge him before getting to know him.

Donnie is a pretty easy-going guy. He takes pleasure in the little things in life. For instance, this is typical of Donnie: "Today, one girl told me I had a great smile. It made me feel great!"

Donnie and the other Kids make a conscious effort to help others. Donnie has a keen interest in producing other bands and currently is lending a helping hand to his brother Mark. "I have a new project in the works with my little brother—Marky Mark and the Funky Bunch," reveals Donnie, excitedly. "Danny just produced a single for him. I just produced a single. Peter Work (New Kids On The Block road manager who also manages a hot New York rap group called the Def Duo) produced a single. Maurice Starr's going to produce two singles."

When Donnie isn't working hard rehearsing and performing with the New Kids and producing other acts, he likes to snooze. He admits that he really misses sleeping late. "It's so nice to be back home in my old bed," he says dreamily. Aside from getting a little homesick once in a while, Donnie has no complaints. He loves being one of the New Kids On The Block, is truly dedicated to the group, and is keeping a wide-awake eye on the New Kids' bright and super future!

DANIEL W. WOOD

FAMILY AND SCHOOL LIFE

I would say I'm a nice guy sometimes…ambitious… determined…lazy sometimes," says Daniel William Wood. Danny is what you'd call a modest fella. Fans would probably want to substitute those adjectives with gorgeous, sweet, sensitive and kind! Any way you look at it, Danny Wood is simply irresistible!

It was time for great rejoicing when Daniel William Wood entered this world, crying and kicking, on May 14, 1970. Elizabeth (Betty) and Daniel Wood, Sr., were extremely happy to welcome their first son into their family. Danny not only had loving parents to take care of his every need, but he also had three older sisters— Bethany, Melissa and Pam—to keep an eye on him.

Soon after Danny's birth, brother Brett and baby sister Rachel were born to complete the Wood family. Now, Danny cheerfully kept his two younger siblings company and played with them every day. Danny's favorite childhood memory is "when my little sister Rachel was born."

Though Danny admits to getting into some mischief when younger, his mom insists that he was delightful and well-behaved. Janet Macoska

The Woods lived (and they still do) in the primarily Irish-Catholic section of Dorchester in Boston. When Danny was growing up, making ends meet was no easy task for the family. "My father is a mailman and my mother is an administrative assistant for the Boston School Committee," says Danny.

"Sharing" was an essential principle that the Wood kids learned right from the start. Danny shared a room with his younger brother Brett. They both slept on bunk beds—Brett on the top and Danny on the bottom. Until recently, Danny was still coming home from touring and collapsing on his bottom bunk with great delight. Now, the Woods' home is being remodeled, and some rooms are being added for more comfort and space.

Danny also attended St. Ann's church regularly with his family. This was a special treat for Mr. and Mrs. Wood because they got to watch all of their lovely children sing in the church choir.

When the time came for Danny to start school, his parents learned that he would be bused out of his neighborhood to William Monroe Trotter School in Roxbury. The Woods supported the busing plan, believing it would be a good opportunity for their older son to learn about other cultures and races. Danny got into mischief now and again, but for the most part his mom says that he was delightful and well-behaved.

Danny was a ray of sunshine in other people's lives as well. His teachers were very fond of him and gushed only compliments. Mrs. Wood told a teen magazine about a teacher's prediction: "I remember when he was in the second grade—one of the teachers told me that he was going to be a heartbreaker," recalls Mrs. Wood with great pride. "She was sure of this because of his big brown eyes." That teacher was right! Millions of gals have fallen in love with Danny's soft-brown eyes!

Another adorable thing about Danny is his incredibly fabulous smile! The Wood family used to say Danny had a "Howdy Doody smile." Everyone likes the tiny dimples Danny has near the corners of his mouth. It's a smile that melts hearts everywhere!

Likable Danny had no trouble making friends at his school. He hit it off almost immediately with another kid named Donnie Wahlberg who was also bused in from Dorchester. The Wahlbergs' and the Woods' houses weren't within walking distance, but Danny and Donnie spent a lot of time together at school.

Danny had friends of many races and backgrounds. Some of his black friends introduced Danny to the sounds of rhythm and blues. Danny and Donnie spent many afternoons watching their pals' street dancing moves, and both of them started to pick up on this funky dance style.

Aside from dancing and music, Danny still maintained an interest in singing. He tried out and was chosen to sing in the Trotter School Chorus.

Danny lifts weights, takes his vitamins, and watches what he eats.
Ernie Paniccioli

Mrs. Wood describes the chorus as a really fun "swing" chorus. She also says that Danny expanded his interests into the acting arena. "I can remember him playing the part of Joseph in a play put on by the religion class he attended on Saturday," she recalls. "He was a bit of a ham when he was little." At this point, Danny wasn't really sure what he wanted to do in terms of a career. He liked to be onstage, but he wasn't sure if he wanted to be a singer or an actor. All he knew was that he enjoyed performing and entertaining others.

While in the school chorus, Danny made friends with two brothers—Jonathan and Jordan Knight. Together, they sang their hearts out. However, after rehearsals came to an end, Danny would bid his chorus pals farewell and hook up with his best buddy, Donnie. The two would spend a lot of time just hanging out with some other Dorchester friends doing typical things that young boys do—going to the movies, listening to music, and playing some ball.

Soon, Danny enrolled in Phyllis Wheatley Middle School along with Donnie. Though Danny was always surrounded by plenty of friends, he is someone you could describe as a "man of few words." While others might scream and yell, Danny would quietly evaluate a situation and then express himself calmly. Danny was also known to stand up not only for his rights, but for the rights of his friends as well.

While in middle school, Danny won quite a few awards. An especially significant one was "The Martin Luther King" award. It was awarded in recognition of leadership and was the most impressive award you could get in that class!

On top of being involved with singing and maintaining an excellent report card all through his school years, Danny participated in sports as well. He really enjoyed working up a sweat running track, playing soccer, and, of course, playing basketball. Danny joined the school's track team, as well as a neighborhood track team back in Dorchester. Following in his brother's footsteps, Brett also became very committed to track. Together, the two Woods won a whole heap of trophies!

DANNY'S CHOICE

Staying fit is very important to Danny Wood. One of the things he really enjoyed about running track in school and playing other sports was that they really helped him stay in shape. Besides that, sports are so much fun! Sometimes, Danny and the other Kids vent their pent-up steam by chilling out on the basketball court before a concert.

At the time Danny was approaching high school (he attended Copley Square High School with chum Donnie), breakdancing became the craze. Danny and Donnie had watched and learned some moves from their pals all through school. Now, the whole style of street dancing was becoming popular. Danny always liked to dance, so this opened up another fitness outlet for him. He saw breakdancing as the perfect way to hang out with his friends, while tightening up his muscles.

Danny was more physical, while pal Donnie was more verbal. Together, they had the coolest raps and the moves to wow any audience! Danny and Donnie (and later Jordan) joined the Dorchester Youth Collaborative, an organization in Boston that put on breakdancing shows mostly for other kids. Members of the D.Y.C. would teach other teens some basic hip street-moves of breakdancing. Danny and Jordan worked at a day camp one summer and taught the children the art of breakdancing. Danny was such an exceptional dancer that he went on to win several breakdancing competitions!

Later, in his teen years, Danny found a way to combine the two things that he enjoyed doing so much—rapping and breaking. Danny joined an organization called Rock Against Racism. This group focused its efforts on making people aware of the problems of prejudice in our society.

Danny got the chance to perform onstage, rapping and breakdancing to his heart's content.

Every day, kids all over the world are faced with making a choice. Sometimes it's as simple as studying for a quiz or blowing it off. At other times, it can be as serious as choosing to take drugs or deciding to walk away from them. Since Danny hung out on the streets with his pals, he saw quite a few people—some were his friends—get into trouble with drugs. For a while, Danny tried to ignore the bad vibes all around him, but one day, he decided to put all of his extra energy into school. He aced history class and math, which was his favorite, and even managed to do well in his least favorite subject—English.

"I was always a good student," says the twenty-year-old. "I was captain of the soccer team, but that was no big deal—we weren't that good! I got awards as Best Math Student. And I sang at our high school graduation ceremony—John Lennon's "Imagine." That was the first singing I'd done without the group, so it was kinda scary. But it came out good."

While Danny was getting good grades and preparing for his future, his old buddy, Donnie, came knocking on his door with an opportunity.

Donnie had just auditioned for Maurice Starr and wanted Danny to join the group. After Danny heard about Maurice's project, he felt his heartbeat quicken. Danny was really getting into Rock Against Racism and wasn't sure if he wanted to give it up to pursue this other musical project. Finally, Danny gave in and auditioned for Maurice. After getting a sampling of Danny's moves and hip street-style, Maurice told him that he got the job. Danny was excited—and scared about the future.

Meanwhile, to complicate matters further, Danny got some fabulous news—he had received a full scholarship to Boston University! Danny's parents very much wanted him to go to college.

Before NKOTB, Danny was rapping and breakdancing with a group called Rock Against Racism. Eugene Shaw, Star File

Torn between two dreams, Danny decided to go to college *and* join Maurice's band. Danny entered Boston University, and scheduled daytime classes so he could rehearse with the New Kids at night. Soon, however, it became apparent that he would have to choose between school and the band. Danny's dean called Mrs. Wood to set up a meeting.

Mrs. Wood expected the dean to recommend that Danny quit the band. Instead, he told her that Danny should pursue the musical group and withdraw from college. "He will always be saying, 'What if?'" explained the dean to a shocked Mrs. Wood.

When Danny chose to put college on hold, his parents were quite disappointed, and Danny's father insisted that Danny get a "real" job. So, Danny worked as a courier, delivering airline tickets, but when "Please Don't Go Girl" started getting airplay, Danny quit his job and put all his energy into the New Kids.

31

GETTING IT TOGETHER

In the beginning, before there was a group choreographer, Danny taught the other Kids some stylish street moves and made sure everyone was in step. Danny, influenced by black music and dance, had learned how to move to the groove from his friends, and in no time at all, it was as if Danny's feet had a mind of their own! Danny happily passed on his dancing tips to Donnie, Joe, Jordan and Jon.

While the Kids were getting it together, they relied not only on Maurice and each other for reassurance, but on their families as well. All the Kids' families served as big, solid shoulders to lean on whenever the need arose.

"My biggest message to the fans is always be nice to your mom 'cause she's always there for you and she deserves it!" states Danny with a smile.

Although Betty Wood says she eventually grew to be very supportive of Danny when he decided to stick with the New Kids, she admits that she expected him to become an architect or an engineer. Maybe her prediction isn't so off the mark as Danny has been tossing around the idea of someday becoming a *musical* engineer. You never know!

Well-deserved success came to the New Kids On The Block with the release of their second album, *Hangin' Tough*. Although the Kids had been working hard for several years, many people tagged them as "overnight sensations" and "one-hit wonders." The band and the fans know that neither of those descriptions are true. The New Kids had been working hard for four years before "Please Don't Go Girl" started getting radio airplay. Soon after that break, the New Kids On The Block grabbed the reins and galloped into the future with an incredible succession of hit singles, proving their incredible talents!

Tiffany is credited with giving the New Kids their most important break. As they toured with Tiffany all across America, they started building up quite a huge following of their own. Pretty soon, New Kids On The Block mania was starting to spread. The Kids were getting recognized on the street and needed bodyguards to protect them from overzealous fans. Almost before Jordan, Danny, Donnie, Joe and Jon knew it was happening, "New Kids On The Block" became a household name.

With the New Kids On The Block's newfound success, Danny and the others discovered that there are disadvantages to being famous. Though they adore performing onstage and they consider themselves very lucky to be able to have found something they love to do so early in their lives, they have had to give up a good deal of their privacy.

Imagine walking down the street to the deli to buy a pack of gum and having people recognize you and call out your name. It certainly was strange, but all five of them loved it! It was a great feeling! Their hard work was finally paying off and people were showing their approval.

Although all of the New Kids love talking to fans and signing autographs, sometimes they miss just being those "regular" kids on the block. Also, all of them will nod in agreement when the topic of sleep comes up. Sleeping late is something each of the New Kids really misses, though Danny claims that he usually wakes up before anyone wakes him up.

After they finished touring with Tiffany, the Kids embarked on their own Hangin' Tough Tour. Show after show sold out lickety-split. Fans just couldn't seem to get enough of their faves, so, they tried to get tickets for as many shows as possible when the New Kids hit their

Both Danny and Donnie made a conscious decision to not get involved with drugs. Chris Mackie

town. Some devoted admirers even followed the band to other states. The Kids were receiving an unbelievable amount of mail and photos of fans from all over the nation. Forget about first base! The New Kids On The Block had hit a grand slam home run!

THE RIGHT STUFF

Although Danny loves to perform, he admits that he sometimes gets nervous before going onstage before thousands of fans. "When they give our shows a lot of hype, I'll get scared and feel those butterflies in my stomach," he says with a big grin.

But as soon as Danny runs out onto the stage with the other Kids, he's immediately at ease! Hearing the screams from the audience helps Danny to put on a great show! If you've seen Danny's def breakdancing routine onstage, you know that when he performs, Danny is a real dynamo! As a matter of fact, the rest of the Kids nicknamed Danny "Puff McCloud," supposedly because Danny does things in a puff or gust of energy.

This chocolate-eyed New Kid says that he lives for performing onstage and is concerned about how the Kids perform during each and every show. After a performance, all of the New Kids get together and discuss what worked really well—and what didn't. Although the shows are choreographed and rehearsed, there is always room for some improvising. Just before a show, for instance, it's not uncommon for Danny or one of the other New Kids to suggest a new dance step. The other Kids check out the move backstage and if they all agree, the Kids try it that night. That's one of the reasons why each New Kids concert is so very unique!

The Kids find that a good time to talk things over and discuss the future is when they're on the tour bus. Currently, Jon and Jordan travel on one bus, while Donnie, Joe and Danny travel on the other. In the beginning, things weren't quite as comfy.

The Kids' first tour bus was inexpensive and unreliable. The first week of the New Kids' tour, the bus broke down about five times! Once, the wheels got stuck in the mud and a tractor had to come pull it out. The Kids laugh when they reminisce about the old days.

Now, their tour buses are reliable, comfortable, spacious, and they have Nintendo. All of the New Kids are big Nintendo fans!

"Our tour buses are *just* like home—living room, VCR, stereo, refrigerator, bathroom, beds," explains Danny. "We love it."

While on the bus, the Kids play video games, talk about upcoming shows, fiddle with their keyboards (Danny practices on his Korg synthesizer) and eat a lot! "But we mostly sleep," says Joe. "The motion of the bus rocks you to sleep anyway. It's nice."

Sometimes, the New Kids get pent-up riding in the

Danny says he likes traveling because it gives him a chance to meet new people and make new friends. Ernie Paniccioli

tour bus, and have to let off some of this trapped energy once they reach their destination! Danny, Donnie, Joe, Jon and Jordan have had their share of fun with food fights and paint pellet guns. Once, they bombed their crew's tour bus with smoke bombs! They say that these "events" are never planned and just happen.

As far as who the tidiest Kid is, the others agree that Jonathan is the neatest. "Donnie, Danny and Joe have one tour bus and Jordan and I the other," explains Jonathan. "I hate messy things, so I pretty much keep all of us clean. Jordan's not too messy. We all have our own closets and stuff." Says Joe with a laugh, "Donnie's probably the messiest, but we try to influence him to be more tidy, ha!"

Each of the Kids likes being on the road for different reasons. Danny likes traveling because it gives him a chance to meet new people and make new friends. He says that a lot of musicians dislike being on the road, but he feels that it's a great opportunity to meet some neat people. Some of them show the Kids around town. "I think I've gotten to know people in every town in the world," says Danny. "It's cool!"

One of Danny's favorite places is New York City. Some of his favorite foods are spicy—especially Mexican food, and he thinks there are a lot of great restaurants in the Big Apple. However, the place that takes first place with the Kids is their hometown—Boston.

Since the New Kids are constantly together, it's natural that they have some disagreements, but they try to get any hard feelings out in the open immediately. If somebody's upset, they all try to work out the problem.

Whatever the problem, the New Kids are like brothers and care for each other very much. Since they all have brothers and sisters, the Kids know how to get along with others rather well. "More important to us than our success or anything, though, is that we're good friends," says Danny. "I think we'll be friends forever."

DANNY DATA

Danny Wood is the type of guy who really cares about his fans. If he sees some fans waiting outside of the Woods' home in Dorchester, it is typical of Danny to go out and say "What's up?" In the past, he's even walked out of his house and given fans autographed NKOTB photos! What a sweetheart! Danny feels that one of the best things about being in the music business and a part of the New Kids, is the fact that you get the opportunity to meet lots of different kinds of people.

Danny's considerate and polite nature results from the way he was raised. He truly is a nice person, so, it makes sense that one of Danny's dislikes is unfriendly people. He just can't understand how some people could be so mean to others. All of the New Kids are well-mannered and extremely friendly. Every chance they get, they try to thank their fans and let them know how much they care.

On a more personal level, Danny describes himself as "stubborn, determined and easygoing." Jordan says that Danny is the type of guy who doesn't stop until the job is done. Joe says that Danny may seem quiet, but don't let that fool you. "He has his moments!" exclaims Joe. Jon describes Danny as a good and reliable guy—a rock-solid type. Finally, Donnie says that sometimes Danny is laid back and sometimes he's wild 'n' crazy! "He gets in conservative moods and then in crazy moods," says Donnie. "We keep waiting for him to dress like a Wall Street stockbroker, and then the next day a punkrocker."

Danny is also very sentimental. He once said that his most prized possession is the time he spent with his mom while growing up. Danny still has fond feelings for a teddy bear puppet that his mom gave him when he was a tot. For his birthday last year, one of the presents Betty sent Danny was a brand new teddy bear. What about his lucky charm? Danny says that his good luck charm is his Tigger the Tiger—a stuffed animal that he keeps on the tour bus.

As far as what characteristics he looks for in a girl, Danny is a real romantic guy who likes girls who are "nice, cute, funny and easygoing." It would also be great if that special girl liked scary movies, travel, playing sports, and of course, dance, dance, dance! Danny's idea of a perfect date is "just spending time with a special girl, getting to know each other."

Among some of Danny's favorite things are: playing basketball, R & B and rap music, Maurice Starr's music, math, writing songs, performing, *The Cosby Show, America's Most Wanted,* Hawaii, the song "Endless Love," actress Cher, roast beef, Mexican, Italian and Chinese food, water, the movies *The Terminator, Stand By Me,* and *Star Wars,* the expressions "I'm outta here," and "Hang tough," meeting people and working out!

Some of Danny's least favorite things are: cruel people, prejudice, being in a rush, being late and people who badmouth the New Kids.

Although Danny has heard the screams of excited fans before, sometimes, he still blushes when a girl yells his name. He's extremely modest about his good looks and—get this—he thinks his head is too square and he's too short! There are thousands of gals all over the world who think you're just perfect, Danny!

Since the Kids are on the road so much, they don't really have time for a leisurely game of basketball or baseball anymore. All of the Kids are athletic, so they'll squeeze in a game after rehearsal, before a sound check or whenever there's a bit of free time. If their hotel doesn't have a fitness center, the Kids will often take to a nearby playground or they'll rent out a school gym close to that night's venue.

Spending time at home with his family and friends still tops Danny's list of favorite leisure time activities. Chris Mackie

Danny has always been concerned about eating healthy and working out. If you happen to wander into the health club at a hotel where the Kids are staying, you just may find Danny working out there. (A New Kids' pal got him interested in body building.) Danny is quick to add that he won't turn into a "muscle-head" and get totally obsessed with lifting weights. He is, however, happy being fit and healthy.

When Danny takes off his shirt at a New Kids concert, fans can feast their eyes on a well-toned, robust body, but Danny says it wasn't always so. "I was always the smallest kid in class till about the 11th grade and I'm still short," he recalls. "I remember one time when I was little, there was this one kid who would pick on me. He was kinda fat and bigger than me and I would usually just walk away. But one day it just got to be too much and I punched him in the mouth."

Rest assured that Danny takes all his vitamins and watches what he eats when the New Kids are on the road. "I just like a good healthy meal like spaghetti and meatballs," says Danny. (Sometimes Danny's mom will travel with the Kids on the road just to make sure!) Staying healthy and fit is one way to keep from getting sick while the band is on tour.

Danny's mother says that her son has weights in the house that he uses when he's back in Boston, and that working out is something Danny likes to do to relax. Danny enjoys spending time at home with his family away from the public eye. In fact, rather than attending glitzy parties and rubbing elbows with other stars, all of the New Kids like to kick back at home in Boston with friends and family doing "regular" stuff such as reading, watching television and sleeping!

Danny not only knows the value of fitness, but the importance of a good education as well. Danny is currently getting some college credit for the education and experiences he is absorbing while traveling all over the world on tour with the New Kids. According to Danny, if the adventures of New Kids On The Block ever come to an end, he says that he very well may go back to college. He hopes that the New Kids will keep going strong, and in the meantime, he'll be sticking with and loving the New Kids forever and ever!

If this bright New Kid does go back to college, he says that he'd probably major in engineering. Danny says that when the Kids are working in the studio, he's very curious about every knob on the control board. He also hopes to continue writing songs and helping other young up-and-coming bands. In fact, Danny teamed up with two other New Kids who also are interested in helping other bands—Donnie and Jordan. After tossing around the name "Mice Posse," the trio decided on calling themselves the Crickets.

The Crickets stay behind the scenes, writing, producing and engineering. Danny, Donnie and Jordan have already succeeded in launching a No. 1 hit song—"I'll Be Your Everything." Jordan had written most of the song when he asked Tommy Page (one of the New Kids'

Danny's second grade teacher told Mrs. Wood that Danny would be a real "heartbreaker" someday. Ernie Paniccioli

opening acts on their Hangin' Tough tour) if he wanted to record it on his upcoming album. Tommy was thrilled with the prospect. So, Danny, Donnie, Jordan and Tommy worked on the music together. In addition to "I'll Be Your Everything," the Crickets also helped Tommy with the song "Turn On The Radio."

For over a year now, Danny's been practicing playing the keyboards, and he's getting mighty good at it. Dynamic Danny is always on the go! Says pal Donnie, "We put our foreheads together before every show, hoping that some of Danny's energy will rub off—not to mention his great dancing." Word!

PART 3

NEW KIDS RULE

ONSTAGE

If you've ever had the pleasure of seeing the New Kids On The Block live onstage, you have some idea about all of the time and energy the Kids put into one of their shows! Danny, Donnie, Jordan, Joe and Jonathan love to perform and entertain their fans—and it shows! Each and every New Kids' performance is one-of-a-kind because the Kids like to get personal with the audience. They'll often chat and crack jokes onstage. Sometimes, there's even a bit of wrestling involved!

During many of their Hangin' Tough shows, the Kids invited a fan onstage during the song "Cover Girl." The Kids like to involve the audience as much as they can. At times, Joe's lovely sister Tricia or one of the other members' siblings will join the Kids onstage, too! All in all, every New Kids' show is full of surprises and excitement galore!

One of the things that makes being a New Kid so enjoyable is all the fun that Donnie, Danny, Jordan, Jonathan and Joe have together. Mixed with all of the hard work, there are times when the New Kids can play and be, well, kids!

The New Kids On The Block have had numerous opening bands, some of which were Tommy Page, The Cover Girls, Sweet Sensation, Bobby Ross Avila and Perfect Gentlemen. If you've attended a New Kids' show, and ever wondered why something just wasn't right, then here's your chance to find out! You see, the New Kids—especially Danny and Donnie—love to play pranks on the opening acts. So, if you didn't understand why the ladies in Sweet Sensation couldn't remove their microphones from their stands, now you will. It's because those frisky Kids taped the mikes to the stands so the girls couldn't get them off! During that show in particular, Joe and Donnie even went so far as to put on wigs and hats and come out onstage and dance during Sweet Sensation's set! Some perceptive fans recognized the dancing Kids right off the bat.

When The Cover Girls toured with the Kids, they also had some fun—New Kids' style! On their Hangin' Tough tour, the New Kids had a six-foot high stage that they took along with them to each venue. The front of the stage had grates that you could put your hands right through. When The Cover Girls wore pumps, they'd stay toward the back of the stage for fear of getting their high heels stuck in the grates. When they wore flat shoes or boots, they could sing at the front of the stage. When the girls were dancing on the grates, mischievous Donnie and Danny would go under the stage and grab their feet and hold them down while they were trying to dance. It must have been hard for The Cover Girls to keep a straight face while performing!

Do the opening acts ever get even? You bet! At one show, the spunky gals from Sweet Sensation devised a plan to get back at the Kids for all those crazy pranks they played on them. If you saw the New Kids on their last tour, you know that they end with "Hangin'

Tough.'' Toward the end of the song, Donnie climbed onto a suspended ramp and hung above the audience. Well, this time, all of the Kids climbed onto the ramp. Suddenly, Sweet Sensation and some crew members ran onto the stage and started throwing food at the New Kids! The New Kids laughed as pieces of cake bounced off of them. Talk about surprises!

According to Donnie, one of the most memorable New Kids' shows was the first time the band ever performed. The Kids debuted at a prison on Deer Island in Massachusetts. All the Kids were nervous and when it was Jordan's turn to step up to the front of the stage and sing, he was too shy to come forward. He sang from the back of the stage. However, the audience didn't seem to notice any of the butterflies that were flying around in the New Kids' tummies. Donnie says that the crowd loved them and it was a wild experience!

Jordan was so shy at the New Kids' debut performance, he would only sing from the back of the stage. Todd Kaplan, Star File

LOVIN' NKOTB FOREVER

After the Hangin' Tough tour, the New Kids had some time off. They all went back to Boston to relax and be with their families. Donnie likes to ride around beautiful Boston in his jeep with a friend and listen to bands such as Public Enemy or Big Daddy Kane. Danny likes to play some ball with his buddies and chill out at home, catching up on the latest in family happenings. Generally, the Kids all like to do mellow things such as going to the movies and sleeping! On the road, the boys miss simple things in life, such as snoozing in their own beds, guzzling milk from their refrigerators and enjoying a hearty home-cooked meal.

You can bet your fave New Kids' poster that when the New Kids On The Block are back in their hometown, Boston fans know about it. Many know where the Kids live, and cruise by every so often in hopes of catching a glimpse of their favorite New Kid. How does the average NKOTB fan do this when chances are she's not old enough to have a driver's license? Well, she gets a bunch of her pals together and they rent a limo for their New Kids quest, that's how!

When the Kids drive up to their houses, there usually are some fans there anxiously waiting for them. Many times, the Kids will stop and chat with their fans and sign T-shirts, photos, jackets and whatever else. Says Donnie, "I want all of our fans to know, if they ever need a friend, we're here."

Sometimes, the New Kids miss being just "average" guys. They miss being able to walk through a mall and shop for jeans. They miss strolling down the street to get a snow-cone from the neighborhood ice cream truck. They can't do simple stuff like that because they often get mobbed and chased by screaming fans who just want to see their idols up close. They need bodyguards (such as Bizcut and Robo) to make sure things don't get out of hand when they're signing autographs. It's all the price of stardom and the New Kids know this.

So, in order to be able to stroll through a crowd without getting noticed, the New Kids do what many, many celebrities (such as Michael Jackson) have done—they put on a disguise! Recently, Donnie and Danny were spotted wandering through a pack of fans, believe it or not, as a couple! To hide their identities, Donnie plopped on a big, fuzzy blond wig, slipped into a dress and put on a nice shade of red lipstick, while Danny put on a wig, a hat and dark shades, and penciled in a mustache and beard! So, the next time you see an out-of-the-ordinary couple walking past you, better take a closer look!

Although most fans of the New Kids On The Block are female, there also are some avid male fans out there who groove to the funky NKOTB beat! When Danny, Donnie, Jon, Jordan and Joe look out into the crowd and see a boy in the audience, it makes them feel really super. "It's also nice when guys are supportive, too," says Donnie. "A lot of times with young guy groups, other guys tend to be jealous and don't give them a chance, but a lot of guys support us and that's very important. 'Cause when we're doing a show, and we see a guy waving his fist or cheering or singing along with us, that's real inspiring. It means that people are judging us for our music and our abilities—it's nice."

Since the Kids don't like it when people judge them just by the way they look and dress, they certainly don't judge their fans on appearances alone. Sure, a pretty face catches their eye, but the Kids know that it's what's inside that counts.

Since the New Kids receive thousands of pieces of mail everyday, they need a fan club office to sort through each letter and package. All of the Kids' moms got together and set up an Official NKOTB Fan Club. The moms head the club and many of the Kids' sisters and brothers work there. Danny's dad, a postman, often transports the sacks of mail to the fan club office.

All of the New Kids receive immense support and encouragement from their parents and siblings. In fact, sticking together has brought all the individual families closer into one, big happy New Kids family! "I wouldn't be anywhere without my parents or brothers and sisters —they have just been great through all of this," reveals Donnie. "I admit that I miss my mom when I'm out on the road, and when she shows up for a show, I can't help but to run up to her and give her great a big kiss! I know it sounds corny, but she's the greatest!"

Although the Kids adore all the thoughtful presents that fans send them for such special events as birthdays and Valentine's Day, they have enough space in their rooms for only so many. Gifts range from chocolates to ceramic Shar-Pei dogs (Jon has a Shar-Pei who travels with the Kids on the road) to homemade T-shirts to jewelry. When the office is really overflowing, the Kids donate some of the toys and stuffed animals to local Boys' Clubs in the urban Boston area. The Kids know that there are lots of needy children out there and they're willing to lend a big helping hand!

AROUND
THE WORLD

One of the things that Donnie, Danny, Jordan, Joe and Jon like about being New Kids is the fact that they get to go to foreign places that they wouldn't otherwise be able to visit. That's why when the New Kids got word that they'd be embarking on a United Kingdom (U.K.) tour in May 1990, all five of them kicked up their heels in delight! The fact that the Kids would be performing at such huge venues as Wembley Stadium in London was proof that the Kids were really going places! Other stars who have performed at Wembley include George Michael and Tina Turner!

When the Kids arrived in London's Heathrow Airport, you can bet that they were welcomed with open arms—400 of them! Nearly 200 fans were on hand awaiting the New Kids entrance. Journalists were comparing the incident to the excitement stirred by The Beatles back in the '60s. Although you would think that things would be a bit looser in England and that the Kids wouldn't get recognized that much, it didn't happen that way. The Kids are loved deeply all over the world! British fans scrambled after the Kids in hopes of getting an autograph and a smile.

Although lots of U.K. teens adore the New Kids, some people do not. Reportedly, a man called the Columbia Records' London office with this solemn message: "I'm going to destroy those wimps." Can you imagine? The New Kids had to triple their security after their first night in London, but with Bizcut, Robo and the extra security protecting them, the Kids could rest somewhat easy.

After bidding their London fans farewell, the New Kids packed up and headed north to Edinburgh, Scotland. There, the Kids took in the visual splendor of the green countryside and chatted with scores of Scottish fans. The Kids were so excited that they spent that whole night hanging out of their hotel room windows rapping to all the delighted gals below. The five Boston babes were jet-lagged, but they didn't mind in the least! "We love our British fans and we're going to give them the best shows they've ever seen!" promised Jonathan.

After Scotland, it was on to Manchester. However, luck just was not on their side. When the Kids marched onto the stage in Manchester, England, they were teeming with energy. As the Kids broke into their first song, an enthusiastic fan threw a red rubber boot up on the stage. Suddenly, Danny stepped on the boot, lost his balance and fell down. He managed to finish up the first song, but by the second song, Danny had to be helped off the stage. After his injury was carefully checked backstage, it was concluded that Danny had a seriously sprained ankle. Under doctor's orders, Danny had to stay off his feet for three weeks. Danny flew back home to Dorchester and began nursing his ankle back into tip-top shape for the New Kids' American tour. Meanwhile, back in the U.K., Danny's bandmates carried on the show.

When asked how he felt about going to the U.K. before the Kids left the U.S., Danny exclaimed happily, "It's going to be dope! (*Dope* is New Kids' slang for great, fabulous, outtasight, etc.) We're going to love it!" Considering Danny's fondness for travel, meeting people and making friends, you can imagine his disappointment after learning that he couldn't continue the U.K. tour. Nevertheless, Danny is a team player and he knows that it is very important that his ankle heal properly and quickly—especially considering all that fancy footwork he does onstage!

The New Kids On The Block's current tour, sponsored by Coca-Cola, is called the Magic Summer '90

Danny has been known to wear a disguise in order to stroll through a crowd without being recognized. Ernie Paniccioli

Tour. The Kids will be singing some smashing tracks from their new album, *Step By Step.* Opening for the Kids this time around are Tommy Page, Perfect Gentlemen and Rick Wes—the latest Maurice Starr discovery. The Kids have been working on some fantastic new dance steps, and have all been practicing playing different instruments. What you can expect on this hot tour is a lot of surprises and plenty of electrifying performances! The Kids kicked off the sold-out Magic Summer Tour on June 24. What a wonderful school's-out-and-summer's-here treat!

The Kids also filmed their very first commercial for Coca-Cola early this spring. Check it out and it's obvious that the Kids had barrels of fun hamming it up for the camera!

TAKING IT
STEP BY STEP

The New Kids have disproved the forecast that they were "one-hit wonders" and a "flash-in-the-pan" band a long time ago. With the immediate success of their latest album, *Step By Step,* the Kids should be around for quite some time to come. The album, recorded in various hotel rooms while the Kids were on the road last year, features all original songs—some co-written by the Kids. Though Maurice Starr produced the album, this time Jordan and Danny assisted their mentor when it came to some important production decisions. The Kids were thrilled to have this input, and learned quite a bit from their hands-on experience. When asked about how *Step By Step* is different from their previous releases, Danny says, "It's still music that we like to do. When we did *Hangin' Tough,* that was two years ago. We were a little bit younger then, and now we're a little bit older. So, I guess you could say it sounds older."

Although the Kids have shown the world that they are multi-talented, some journalists still fail to recognize this. Some say the band isn't singing about anything important and that the Kids just perform sweet, bubblegum music. The Kids dislike being categorized and claim that their music is constantly changing and that they have more than one message.

Donnie thinks that some of the press have given the Kids a bad rap. "I just think they haven't given us a chance," he begins. "I could shrug it off and say that respectability comes with longevity. That's what people say. The Beatles had trouble when they were younger. The Rolling Stones had trouble with the press when they were younger. But I don't mind the press knocking me—as long as they knock me in the correct way. Knock me about the truth. Don't knock me about nothing—knock me about something."

The New Kids' message is simple—keep an open mind. In addition to keeping an open mind, the Kids have warned children about the dangers of doing drugs. The Kids didn't just sit around one day and decide to take on a clean-cut, drug-free image. They all have lost friends to drugs and know how dangerous they are, and they make their firm stand against drugs known in hopes of reaching teenagers all over the world and convincing them to "Just say no!"

"We just want to show kids that being an individual is the best thing you can be," explains Donnie. "Don't give in to peer pressure and stuff like that. 'Cause no matter what happens, it's you against the world. We just want everyone to do things for themselves, learn things for themselves—and do what your heart tells you to do!"

The New Kids are very concerned about the problems in the world today. They have taken a stand against drugs and racism, and have donated money and their services to many charities. As "National Spokespeople" for Cerebral Palsy, they have ridden at Bike-a-thons and at this year's annual United Cerebral Palsy Telethon, the Kids not only performed, but donated all the profits from the sales of their single "This One's For The Children" from the Kids' 1989 Christmas album, *Merry, Merry Christmas* to UCP! Also, the telethon, which took place on January 20 and 21, set up a New Kids 900 phone line, where all the profits—at $5 a call, went to UCP. The phone line raised $200,000 in just two days! The Kids plan to participate in the telethon next year and are hoping to double the money raised! In fact, Donnie has challenged the members of New Edition to play a celebrity basketball game with the New Kids, with all of the proceeds going to United Cerebral Palsy.

ON THE HORIZON AND INTO THE '90s

The New Kids On The Block have come a long way since 1985! They've got four albums under their belt, countless hits and plenty of awards! The Kids were honored with two American Music Awards and, more recently, three Boston Music Awards. Boston honored their five babes in the categories of *Outstanding Pop/ Rock Single* for "I'll Be Loving You (Forever)," *Outstanding Video* for "Hangin' Tough," and the highly prestigious *Act of the Year* award! Way to go, New Kids!

To many people's dismay, there were some boos heard from the supporters of the hard rock act, Aerosmith, when the Kids got up to receive their awards at the Boston Music Awards. Donnie addresses the situation with classic New Kids' style. "Rock 'n' roll is being stereotyped as a thing for white guys with long hair and being about sex, drugs and rock 'n' roll," says the unofficial New Kids' spokesperson. "That's not what it's about. If I want to make music that's positive and that's about girls and about love, then that's my freedom of expression. I don't have to get up onstage and play heavy metal or whatever. Rock 'n' roll is about being yourself and any rock 'n' roll musician should recognize that and know that."

Although the New Kids have achieved quite a bit these past few years, they still haven't met one of their all-time idols—Michael Jackson. They have met plenty of other people whom they admire greatly. It's still kind of strange to them that they see people on TV and then the next day, those very people are backstage, waiting to be introduced to the Kids in the "Meet And Greet

The message from all of the New Kids is simple—keep an open mind, and don't give in to peer pressure. Larry Busacca/Retna Ltd.

Room." Once, Marv Albert (an NBC sportscaster) walked backstage with his daughters in tow and presented the Kids with official Knicks jerseys. You can bet that Jon, Jordan, Joe, Danny and Donnie were thrilled!

One thing that the New Kids have that many other musicians don't are their own dolls! There are New Kids dolls featuring the Kids that come with typical show clothes as well as in everyday fashions. And each doll really looks like each New Kid. When asked how it feels to have dolls that look like them on toy store shelves everywhere, the Kids agree that it's pretty neat.

"It was weird at first," says Danny. "I couldn't figure out why we were all the same height and then I remembered that all the dolls are made a certain size. I actually get an even bigger kick out of the phone!" That's right! If fans just can't seem to get enough of the New Kids On The Block, then they may be into getting a cool NKOTB phone to gab on. Look for watches, party goods, pillow cases, pajamas and lunch boxes, and don't be surprised if you see a tasty New Kids On The Block breakfast cereal coming up soon, too! Sounds yummy!

Have you heard rumors about New Kids On The Block dancing across the silver screen? It's all true! The New Kids are working with Jon Peters and Peter Guber (this dynamic duo brought us *Batman*) on a flick for Columbia Pictures. As of yet, there is no title, but the script is nearly finished. In the past, Joe hinted that it may be an adventure story set in a foreign country. Danny says that the film will not really be about New Kids On The Block. "The movie is going to be a fact/fiction type of thing," explains Danny. "It's based on New Kids On The Block, but it's going to have a twist to it. It's not going to be like the real story with how we got started and got together." In the meantime, every time something memorable or funny happens, the Kids save it on tape for the movie. Rumor has it that the Kids will be playing themselves and that they'll begin filming soon in sunny Southern California. So, keep your eyes peeled!

And look for the New Kids in animated form every Saturday morning on ABC this fall. Each show will supposedly kick off with a funky New Kids' tune and will conclude with a dynamic New Kids performance. The cartoon will follow the stars as they strive to be just "regular kids." Each story supposedly will feature the New Kids trying to solve a problem for one of their friends or fans. Then the Kids race back to the concert just in time for one more song! What more could you ask for? Each episode will be topped to the brim with fascinating New Kids' capers and antics! Be sure to tune in!

Even with such hectic schedules, the Kids somehow make time for helping other up-and-coming bands. Donnie, Jordan and Danny lent a hand to their buddy Tommy Page and recorded two songs with him (the No. 1 hit single "I'll Be Your Everything" and "Turn On The Radio") when they could have been chillin' on a beach in Hawaii. Donnie sang a duet with Japanese pop sensation, Seiko, and Jordan sang a duet with pal Ana. At the Boston Music Awards, New Kids On The Block introduced a Boston rap band who they think is really happening—Young Nation. Meanwhile, Donnie is in the process of producing his little bro's band, Marky Mark and the Funky Bunch. It's amazing what these Kids can squeeze into a day's work!

All in all, it looks like another New Kids' year! The number of New Kids' fans continues to grow, and the future of the New Kids On The Block seems as peachy and as promising as ever. Twenty years from now, who can say where the Kids will be? Will Donnie be a producer? Will Danny have become an engineer? One thing is for certain, though—the Kids will keep taking a stand against racism and drugs. And all of the guys will be lovin' NKOTB fans forever!

"Not wanting to be on an ego trip or anything—if I can make somebody's day by touching their hand, I'd be a jerk not to touch their hand," says Donnie. "It's so easy. It's not like I have to run twenty miles to make someone's day—I just have to touch them."

The New Kids On The Block really do care! Entertaining people with their music is something that really makes the Kids extremely happy. And to adoring New Kids' fans all across the world, this Boston band's funky fresh beats and rhythms are like rays of sunshine every day!

MUSIC AND VIDEOS

New Kids On The Block (Columbia, April 1986; Re-released 1989)

Tracks: "Stop It Girl" (M. Starr); "Didn't I (Blow Your Mind)?" (W. Hart, T. Bell); "Popsicle" (M. Starr); "Angel" (M. Starr, J. Cappra); "Be My Girl" (M. Starr); "New Kids On The Block" (M. Starr, D. Wahlberg); "Are You Down?" (AJ, E. Nuri, K. Banks, D. Wahlberg); "I Wanna Be Loved By You" (M. Starr); "Don't Give Up On Me" (M. Starr); "Treat Me Right" (M. Starr).

Hangin' Tough (Columbia, March 1988)

Tracks: "You Got It (The Right Stuff)" (M. Starr); "Please Don't Go Girl" (M. Starr); "I Need You" (M. Starr); "I'll Be Loving You (Forever)" (M. Starr); "Cover Girl" (M. Starr); "I Need You" (M. Starr); "Hangin' Tough" (M. Starr); "I Remember When" (M. Starr, E. Kelly, J. Randolph, C. Williams); "What'cha Gonna Do (About It)" (M. Starr); "My Favorite Girl" (M. Starr, D. Wahlberg, J. Knight); "Hold On" (M. Starr).

Merry, Merry Christmas (Columbia, September 1989)

Tracks: "This One's For The Children" (M. Starr); "Last Night I Saw Santa Claus" (M. Starr, A. Lancellotti); "I'll Be Missin' You Come Christmas (A Letter To Santa)" (K. Nolan, M. Starr); "I Still Believe In Santa Claus" (M. Starr, A. Lancellotti); "Merry, Merry Christmas" (M. Starr, A. Lancellotti); "The Christmas Song (Chestnuts Roasting On An Open Fire)" (M. Torme, R. Wells); "Funky, Funky Xmas" (M. Starr, D. Wahlberg); "White Christmas" (I. Berlin); "Little Drummer Boy" (K.K. Davis, B. Onorati, H. Simeone, adaptation by J. Edwards); "This One's For The Children" (Reprise).

Step By Step (Columbia, June 1990)

Tracks: Side One: "Step By Step" (M. Starr); "Tonight" (M. Starr, A. Lancellotti); "Baby, I Believe In You" (M. Starr); "Call It What You Want" (M. Starr); "Let's Try It Again" (M. Starr); "Happy Birthday" (M. Starr, M. Jonzun).

Side Two: "Games" (M. Starr, D. Wahlberg); "Time Is On Our Side" (M. Starr, A. Lancellotti); "Where Do We Go From Here?" (M. Starr); "Stay With Me, Baby" (M. Starr, M. Jonzun); "Funny Feeling" (M. Starr, M. Jonzun); "Never Gonna Fall In Love Again" (M. Starr, M. Jonzun, D. Wood).

Singles: "Step By Step" released 5/90; future singles not announced at press time.

SINGLES

"Be My Girl"
"Stop It Girl"
"Didn't I (Blow Your Mind)?"
"Please Don't Go Girl"
"You Got It (The Right Stuff)"
"I'll Be Loving You (Forever)"
"Cover Girl"
"Hangin' Tough"
"This One's For The Children"
"Step By Step"

MUSIC VIDEOS

"Please Don't Go Girl"
"You Got It (The Right Stuff)"
"I'll Be Loving You (Forever)"
"Cover Girl"
"Didn't I (Blow Your Mind)?"
"Hangin' Tough"
"This One's For The Children"
"Step By Step"

VIDEOCASSETTES

HANGIN' TOUGH (CBS Home Video, 1989)
This 30-minute home video contains interviews and backstage footage as well as videos for the four hits off the *Hangin' Tough* LP: "Please Don't Go Girl," "You Got It (The Right Stuff)," "I'll Be Loving You (Forever)" and "Hangin' Tough."

HANGIN' TOUGH LIVE (CBS Home Video, 1989)
Every New Kids hit off their second LP is performed live in this half-hour-long cassette.

AWARDS AND HONORS

AMERICAN MUSIC AWARDS
—Favorite Pop/Rock Album (*Hangin' Tough*)
—Favorite Pop/Rock Group

BOSTON MUSIC AWARDS
—Outstanding Pop/Rock Single ("I'll Be Loving You Forever")
—Outstanding Video ("Hangin' Tough")
—Act Of The Year

GRAMMY NOMINATION
—Best Music Video (Long Form)

ON TOUR
European and Magic Summer

**Tour
Photos**

Meyer/Fotex/Shooting Star